poetry

Girl In The Empty Nightgown

Eloise Bradley Fink

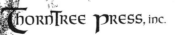

ThornTree Press, inc.

Acknowledgement is given to the following for the first publication
of some of these poems:
Avon Books, Richard Peck, editor, *Poems That Storm Inside My
Head*
Sotheby's International Anthology
Chicago Tribune Magazine

Cover art by Hilda Rubin Pierce
Logo by Laura M. Doyle
Photography by Vicki Grayland
Typography by Patricia Wilson Barnes
Layout by Martin Bartels

Special thanks to David Simonson, editor and publisher, Pioneer
Press, and to John Daiberl

ISBN (Clothbound) 0-939395-02-9
ISBN (Paperback) 0-939395-03-7
Library of Congress Catalog Number: 86-050926

Published in 1986 by
Thorntree Press, Inc.
547 Hawthorn Lane
Winnetka, Ill. 60093

Contents

BIG BEAR SHADOW

He was her guide; she walked
   inside his big bear footprints
through lost centuries
   of Indians in old museums.

He read concert notes to her while Mozart
   moved like amber through the strings.
Bronze autumn cello, yellow pears.
   Small, wheat-slim notes were falling
into her, their sweet
   seeds — swinging.

Art galleries were new, his shadow warm.
   "Impressionist's tonality," he said,
"obtains from techniques of not mixing
   their component hues." He held her
arm while she was walking Renoir fields —
   sun-tasting petals like champagne. Paint
woven in a basket of raw color, thicketed in green,
   a scratch of light, caught in the artist's eye.
Blue afternoons of sun seined in, cooled
   fishing leaves. And seascapes
real as water flowing over canvas, off.
   She breathed an ocean fog beneath
the brush-scraped sky. She watched sun-
   bathing models bask like smiling water-
beds of pink. Except for one, with firm
   breasts puckered, made to hide
behind, for looking carefully out
   to view the artist, while she lay
revealed — no secrets — only deep as dark,
   and black as lace furred over skin.

"I'll find an art appreciation course for you,"
   he said, and bent to kiss her
cheek — not noticing her breasts,
   song-round as birds, watched him.

ONE GREAT BEAR

The two moved into
    each, together — arms
around, their legs cat's cradle
    finding where
they finally belonged
    beyond that valley
of the open tulip.
    They lay there — like one
great bear -- nose quivering
    and loving its own salt
suck-touch. They were an island —
    loaf heaped high in rounded
fur of sleep. They moaned
    their long, low in-out
breath while dream squalls stirred
    and owled through their night.

GIRL IN THE EMPTY NIGHTGOWN

He had watched her slow becoming:
    ample apron of a wife —
warm smell of cinnamon
    about her hair,
with sugar-cookie kisses
    for the children.

Always he was late for the eight-twenty-
    eight — her crisp "good morning"
curling like the smell of bacon
    through the bedroom.

And at night, again, as basic as an egg,
    and looking up at him.
Their way upstairs his hand had
    lightly found her hip —
a yeast bread, round and smooth —
    and when she rumpled into bed,
it was as if a basket
    of clean flannel nightgowns
had been toppled over,
    leaving one dazed, armless sleeve
caught on the edge. Before
    he turned the light out she sat up,
moved close and pulled her legs
    up under, with a pillowness
that made him wish the snow outside
    wall high, moat wide.

But sometimes, only sometimes,
    he remembered that first day —
the forest, how he'd made her move,
    quick flight of feathers.

TWO MIGRANTS —
GREAT GRANDPARENTS

They had come together in a time
    when prairie poor folks
fruited all the fields
    that turned the Midwest
rich. They watched the sweeps
    of great green grain
turn gold and dusty with the musk
    of money, and their arms
were nets
    to haul it in.

When rivers bled with ranch wars,
    they lay watching
harvests of the wheating clouds,
    sun burning through her eyes
and into him. The timber moved,
    doves lifting up the fields
into the sky. They shared the sharp
    bite of new apples,
fire drinking up the dark.
    They hounded moons
across the meadows, till a morning
    wind blew her away like chaff.
The songs she left
    got lost in his guitar.

BRED AND LEFT

My grandmother's
flared hips were flat
and broad as any bread board, serving one loaf
then two others, and another, warm --
round babies left by that tight-torsoed-
expert-switch-blade-dancing-man,
my grandfather.

SWINGING BACK

I sit still, trying on
    my Grandma's face —
here in the mirror — trace her
    eyebrows, gothic arched, above
small grottoes cupping sun. I touch
    the pale petunias of her
cheeks, and, like some misty nest, her
    cloud of hair. Her smile she wore
pulled up like that rope swing
    where all of us would fly high
up and reach out toward the church
    steeple to ring our shoes
against its bell rim —
    while her laugh looped
higher than the bell and brought
    us back into her arms.

A BRIDGE

When she was ten, her father hiked with her
      through timber till the sun burned rivers
down the sky and left small fires glowing
      in the roadside puddles after dusk.

He'd told her how -- when he was seventeen -- no dad
      and seven kids at home, he'd gone to work. No
time for looking at the sunsets then. His life was
      forged inside the Wabash locomotive shop. One day
his right sleeve fed into a gear. The splinted
      arm, thonged onto splintered bone, got stronger
than before, he liked to say, although he'd never
      straighten all his fingers out.

"They should be straight?" he'd asked. "This way
      I get a tighter grip on things; they help me
figure out new ways." He hoped she'd not forget.
      He seemed to try one thing, then look away
and listen -- let machines talk back to him
      and tell him what they needed. People, too.

Years later, one night -- it was three A.M. --
      the Wabash foreman called him, saying
that their bridge down south in Illinois
      was stuck, would not go down.
He took his toolbox, drove two hundred miles
      to listen to a bridge.

THE PLEDGE IN KINDERGARTEN

Like a tricycle with one run-over wheel,
    he spindled toward the playground,
but he raced. He rode inside a body
    with bent spokes. It was not really
his. It rode on his
    curved spine.

When Science read his bones,
    it spelled a dystophy
and taped its label to him.
    Yes, he knew the doctors liked him,
smiling as the needles stuck in deep
    for quick sucks of his blood.

They saved it on their slides,
    in tubes, and sometimes
on hospital sheets. The tests
    and x-rays doctors pledged,
would not help his legs grow,
    but they might find the answers
for another boy someday
    somewhere.

If only he could see
    the boy and know
that he would not like being
    "normal" quite enough
to push the little kids
    in cafeteria lines.
He'd learned to be Red Rover's
    target, though he wouldn't let go
till they'd grounded him.
    The tearing arm.

They'd yell, "Hey, Shrimp!"
    and toss his hat.
He'd laugh and chase them
    back to class to pledge allegiance
to the flag — somewhere
    amid their belt buckles in which
he stood, almost invisible, with liberty
    and justice, yes, for all.

THE MOTHER'S MACHINE

The Sphinx sets all the Singer's wheels
to music -- purring its Industrious
Resolution. It does what it's treadled to --
although it seems to dream
beyond the sand to Niles of mornings,
as it nimbles, quite nearsightedly,
across the pins and agiles waistlines
in and carefuls all around the hems.

Its date embossed, December fifth, in 1882.
The Sphinx, tatooed with gold leaf on black
steel, eyes through the needle's yards
of smooth horizon -- moving
like a desert through its paws.

It does not stop -- except occasionally.
The mother rubs her eyes and sighs;
the bobbin hisses and runs out.

MORNING TIMES

Black morning snow is huddled on the news
    that's waiting to be wedged into the paper-
boy's bicycle basket. Fingers sprung, he lifts
    thick drifts of snow-thin words.
He hides inside his jacket, pedals hard
    to keep his balance, pitches with his good
left arm — prints news across the welcome mats
    on Orchard Lane, delivering it
like fresh baked bread, hot headlines
    black as coffee, waking up the world.

JOEL

Through the reddened eye
    of morning, moody clouds,
he'd slipped into our lives
    like one dropped appleseed.

He flowered long before
    he thought himself
into a tree — his eyes as small
    as seeds that saw into
the centers of his tinkerings,
    or candlefire.

A twist-in at the trunk kept him
    from growing tall, but made
a nest-place cupped for sparrows
    'til they fluffed and flew.

His words surprised the corners
    of his mouth,
made laughter through
    bright leaves.

COMFORTER

Alison was swaddling her
sick cat inside the gingham
pillowcase.

Her cat's eyes were a gingham
blue — and lost behind a sky
they tried to see through.

Yet, it was the cat who'd held her
altogether through geometry
and boys and A's and F's and acne.

Every night inside her billowed
comforter, she told her folded
secrets to those soft triangle

ears — her diary with angled
eyes and parallel whiskers.
But today she brought the pillowcase

home empty from the vet's —
a slim chemise stepped out of.
In the middle of this night

when she turns over, her toes touch
that cozy space that used to curve
inside the comforter on her big bed.

CONCERT IN GRANT PARK

Music was a picnic opened up
    next to the lake, spread out
on blankets, squirreling
    up through the trees. Kids giggled,
gulping cherries while the orchestra
    director traced the music.

White wings ruffled,
    whirring from his sleeves.
Two fat-pie cymbals burst
    and let a dozen doves fly out.

The audience was licking slippery plum
    juice from the edges of their lips —
thick bread and sausages. Their tongues
    were listening to the violinist

slicing thinnest rinds high off the hock.
    Clear silver served the suckling
song — tart apple taste, sharp in their throats
    and up into their ears.

ON MAKING ANGELS IN THE SNOW

Fresh snow prickles quiet
    miles that sleep between them
in the big suburban bed that stretches
    out beyond the city
limits of their caring who
    they might have been
if they had let their separate
    angels arc smooth feathers
intersecting wings across the lace
    words of their pillows.

MONEY

You've got
to have
enough
to begin
with
out
side of
what you
need to get
by with
and then
invest
the rest
resist
the thought
of it;
insist
it ceases
to exist
for you
he said,

you know
like love.

THE WOOLEN AFGHAN

He was never angry with her,
    he declared. And broke
the chair. She waited, hating
    twenty years of hurting
her voice gave him with its mulled
    again I'm sorrys.

He ran out. She stumbled up
    the stairs. The children lay
on beds as if they'd drowned
    were wretched out
on a beach. One lolled a foot —
    still ankle-deep in sleep.

The wind outside was flogging night —
    and surly in the streets, rough-
jamming gusty elbows grappling in the
    chimney, brusquing through the house
and out and over trees, as if it bullied
    all the prairie,
owning it completely, as an ocean
    running over.

Then he banged the door shut, locked
    them in.
And when he fell
    asleep upon the sofa,
she went downstairs,
    coaxed his wet shoes off
and pulled the afghan up
    across his shoulders.

HE DIDN'T LOOK AT HER

Outside the window it was raining.
　　He watched clouds
wave-wash the far horizon
　　of black trees.

Although he'd memorized the bedded touch
　　of her against him, felt her
breathing throat and breast,
　　it was as if he were still twelve,
had stopped outside to see a dirt road
　　filling up with rain.
Again, he straddled his
　　old bike — the cold bar
throbbing hard between his legs —
　　and ridged the front tire
back and forth and back
　　until he was inside
that spring-delicious road
　　again.

P.S.

Outside a blur
   of lilacs
moved against the fog —
   blind-grey as distances
that groped between
   the two inside.

He pulled his trousers up
   and turned away
to zip his fly.
   He lurched into his coat,
remembered, turned again,
   tight-pursed his lips
to measure one dispensable
   quick kiss.

LIKE SPRING

"Damn right, I had a long lunch
     with her. Yes, we laugh a lot.
She's always new. She's like . . .
     like Spring."
He smudged the fogged-up window.
     Rain splashed on the wind-
shield as the wipers waxed black
     arcs across the night.
The light turned red like dark
     gashed open, but he didn't stop.

"This fuckin' muck!" Tires screamed.
     He jerked the wheel.
The truck jammed brakes and ripped
     their Buick -- jaw from skull.

The rain was all around her
     now, but thicker, cold.

The rain was licking up the leaves,
     and thirsting high above
her somewhere, slapping shingles,
     bleeding green through grass
and drinking night up, as her legs
     filled up with cold black rain
where she lay drowning
     all his words inside.

MUSIC-GO-ROUND

Their father was the key.
He wound his laughing music box
of children on the merry-

go-round.
"Come on, Mother,
come over the bridge,"

the children called.
But she had staggered music
in him. Singing Saturdays did not

belong to her. She waved them on.
Though they had learned to borrow
him from his new world,

she did not know quite how to
say there were no
whole notes left for her,

no open lips to round
hellos. The numbered
months alone had numbed her

with the strum cicadas
make to rock the night
to sleep.

She waited in the park, leaves
listening to the sun melt autumn
off the trees.

BICYCLE TRIP

The mother pulled her grin so straight
   she couldn't let it go.
"G'bye! I'll call you, Mom.
   A day or two." Her son
limped quickly off the porch.
   The other sophomores moved carefully
as astronauts through serious
   cold of three a.m. —
checked tires, packs strapped,
   bolts tight.
She waved. His knee-light
   ground swift orange circles,
orbiting away and pulling
   miles as he
slipped in between the flash-
   light fingers of the dark.

BLUE SCISSORS

Waking the dark,
she called out, "Mommie, Mommie!"
Nodding wind clicked branches,
gestured wibbley fingered witches --
silhouettes half sleep.

"See? There. The trees are writing
on my curtains!"
Shadows cut moon gingerbread
like paper dolls
with bright blue scissors.

UP XYLEM LADDERS

All winter only feather silence there
    between them, resting white and muffling
corners into coves and whispering stillness
    all along the sills with no
words anywhere to touch, to say that they
    were still alive through snow.

Tonight he shouted, threw
    a book, was sorry.
Winds were shredding cold. Ice cracked
    like tight ripe melons split,
slashed open with erupting
    seeds of black night rain
that clacked against
    the window, desperate fingers
pebbling on the pane: a love
    not quite forgotten.

Rain climbed up the xylem ladders of the oaks,
    moved high into their puckered
rose-tight buds screwed round
    their black-stick finger ends —
with growing nippled out
    against the fresh, whorled air.

His arms around — her ear, snow-deep against
    her pillow, heard warm rain pumped
through her veins, like patient
    miles of pilgrim feet — or yet,
almost like mud splashed up
    through toes — toward spring.

FATHER

The children laughed last year
    when he installed the Sure-Grip-
Twin-Trick-Lock-and-Burglar-System --
    magic circle drawn around their life

till he ran out one night, forgot
    to close the door. Their master
key was lost, and no one quite remembers
    why they used to lock the house.

MYTH

In the flare of red November leaves, we cheered
    the President-elect, and suddenly our world
seemed understandable, a stadium where we
    could block the Russians in a scrimmage
that was fair and final as a score.
    We'd grin and go ahead together toward
his New Frontier. Our own young family
    snugged close, tight as petals in a bud.

The President was ours — the country like a family;
    shrill stripes with bursting stars belonged
to us. We could not clap enough; we had to
    watch him, reach out, touch him — even through
our TV screens, and we could read his eyes.
    His Knighthood had survived our storybooks.
She was his queen, a silver candlestick. They
    took us with them, lighting up the world.

In glaring noonlight, he waved love to Dallas.
    He seemed like a furry creature they had
caught. His eyes. He looked out under slant-up brows.
    The flag drank warm November wind.
And then the bullets tearing air and life away —
    and petals falling everywhere — and families,
our own, with no one quite believing anyone
    belonged to anyone. Not anymore.

A jagged sun had scarred the swollen sky. Bare trees
    scraped angry words around the edges. Sirens screamed
for us; dazed headlights smeared dull dandelion blurs
    across the dark cortege. Since then, the night
was never big enough to hide inside. Without the myth
    we might someday let mushroom skies break off.

VISE

Propped against her eyelid,
   night slits open.
Moon squints bright as ground
   glass gritted on the snow
and blown into her eyes.
   The old springs moan
as she turns over, and the cats
   pull nerve ends through their claws —
re-sorting dreams and biting
   on their tails. The bed is vise
enough to hold her in this life
   against his wooden back
while children closed in rooms
   drink sleep like cocoa death.

FOR BEING A MOUSE

The cabin was a place away
    to plan divorce. Bags in,
he had a drink, a Baby Ruth,
    and skimmed the news. He put a dish
of D-con by the fireplace — he'd talk
    tomorrow, closed his door.

The children didn't count in this,
    he'd said. Fire crinkled,
fizzed. Crisp echo of his
    candy wrapper,
nibbling edges off the dark —
    a mouse.

She flipped the light.
    A deer mouse —
fur white under-soft,
    bright facts for eyes.

When sunlight webbed the windows
    he spoke legal algebra.
She looked down at the D-con
    dish, half full.

The mouse climbed up the table,
    walked across his paper,
sneezed a smallest rose bouquet.
    It rubbed its nose;
its foggy fingers printed fine red
    lace across the editorials.

"My paper? Christ. Well,
    come outside."
He lit a cigarette.
    "Don't watch it die."

The mouse scratched halfway up
    the fireplace — arms out,
a crooked cross. It turned and skated
    down the stones, feet stammering.
It crouched behind the bent-up
    ear of paper, held on,
wouldn't let itself tip
    over. Then it circled
in a dance across the headlines,
    stumbled — sprung —
curled up: a picture
    in a bedtime book.

STARS CALLED THEM BY THEIR GIVEN NAMES

Although he asked that she give back
    his rib, he said he'd heard divorce law
usually left that with the wife. Eve only
    asked that he should try remembering.

They waited on a balcony
    outside the judge's chambers.
Both looked up; stars stiffened,
    but she still believed,
a benediction lingered from those
    long-ago left nights
when all the stars had known them —
    called them by their given names.

She'd said that Love was where they'd lived --
    their bare feet teething on the warmth
before the fire -- where mornings found
    tart berries hidden under fern.
He cupped three in his hand for her,
    then kissed the melt of them
along her lips. And rain, like buttons, popped
    on ponds they waded in,
their toes, tin ice. He pulled her
    out and rubbed her feet warm pink.
Wind ran with them and slapped
    the clouds and pushed them
all up-mountain with the marching
    pines — and dreams that raced on stilts
up to the top, where he sat down, just like
    a fox on his own rock. And grinned.

Years hummed with light and talking stars,
    light years away, and only slowly
did he come to see the snake that
    followed him, that led him from
their place. When he looked back,
    their old skies seemed cliche
of summer, all the same. So run.
    Run fast from her.

Her head was trembling with the voices
    he had left to her,
her hands complacent as a plate
    upon her lap.
His legal eyes were set. Lost from each
    other, all their apple trees and lambs
on Eden Hill were lost to both of them
    Their orchards -- choked with apples
no one wanted -- died. Colts skittered off.
    Yet she could not forget their
garden place, how near the stars
    had been. Just then, as they stood
looking up, the stars began to move,
    step down the sky.

He reached out for her, not quite sure.
    Could they run back together, find their place?
A star moved closer, then called out, "Hello,
    down there! Is that you, Adam?"

INJECTION — THIRD TRIMESTER

She was there inside
of him; he'd chosen her
and locked her underneath his rib,
lub-dub together grown.

He'd wombed her in his world
while she made life in shapes of hand-
prints, cerebellum cord, small flutter thrums.
She quickened living through his veins.

At term, he'd said, their family raised, she could
come out, be born, an equal — living next to him.
Still, he resented her, his balding and his own slowed pace,
their children, surly, college-bound.

Break clean. Annul her right to life. He'd womb another
pregnancy. He closed his eyes but shuddered deeply
where the needle stuck. Why had no doctor warned
him he would labor under this injection?

Saline worked, and it was fast. It was
his best solution. God! It burned.
It ulcered holes inside his belly
as the brine convulsed her arms.

She screamed her feet against his womb.
Her soles — she'd tear him up.
Her time was up. "Head down
. . . and out!"

NOT LOOKING BACK

She's left behind his stiff, slammed gate;
    their house fills up with dark. Outside,
blue flowers turn black with dusk; they huddle
    all together like a funeral that won't go home.

TO THE COMMUTER TRAIN — IN SNOW

How many arctic months had wedged between
    him, bold explorer, and the station
now just miles ahead? White days
    with holes slit through for eyes
that stared like stars into the glassy
    bright. He couldn't quite remember
how he'd gotten here. Once happy — wife
    and kids — until this grind of woman-
hunger, changing him to anger as he felt
    its ranting antlered to his brain.

He'd watched the sexy sea begin to move —
    grow wobbly with a herd of walrus
haunches. He had stabbed the water, turned
    it red. The blood in snow like
sherbet of fresh raspberries.
    He tore the fruited flesh
and drank at it until he'd soaked
    his chest and arms. Then, turn about,
small rage of fire red-gnawed the dark
    and nearly ate him up. Black sleep.
When he woke up — as swollen as a bear
    and clumsy with the cold,
his eyes mossed over with the snow —
    he knew he'd only this day left
to free himself or freeze. He tried
    to run, clumped hard through clods
of ice. Far off, he heard the train
    hoots, whistling death away.

Just one more block now, pushing
    through the nine-to-five commuters
racing minutes, leaving in the suburbs
    all the winters of his life.
He'd hide inside the city — not come back —
    and never let cold catch him anymore.

JUSTICE

She couldn't go
with him
he said
and knocked her
down there
on the rail
road platform
skidding cheek
and knees across
old splinters,
clamped himself
in that commuter's
cage, steel-wheeled
away mid-sentence
half-commuted
and committing her
to that hole
family left
behind his
emptied
tracks.

FEBRUARY, IT'S SNOW MAN

Mirage-deep, treading, vague
    as snow, he comes to visit
home. The fence is chain-link lace.
    Up in Victorian eaves, round
sparrows have been nibbling
    gingerbread for years.
Strong porch posts that he built
    still keep the care he spindle-
carved in them, smile-smooth,
    down to the bone.

He takes his turn with children
    while she drives to find
the longest double-feature
    she can hide inside.
He opens up their bright red door
    to count the children,
say their names, as if
    he knew them once.

Cane fireside chairs as "theirs"
    as coffee cups. The fire gone out,
yet, embers left -- strawberry wild --
    as red as kisses burned
in dark. And on the table, left,
    warm sugar cookie hearts --
too crumbly, scorched around
    the edge. This room:
the TV talks where people
    used to. Just as well.
He puts his coat on,
    closes up their Valentine.
Who was it that they
    made it for?

STOPPING ON A SNOWY EVENING

Not wanting to go home, my car drives slowly
        through the village, bright with window
squares, each pasted to black pages of a photo
        album. Scenes of families -- the chosen
ones -- with fathers home to bauble babies,
        carve the roast, and prove the high
school theorems no one else is equal to.
        Framed dreams to light my sleep.

I stop the car beside a large New England
        farmhouse, fenced with privet,
snowed-in smug and private. There,
        the family inside is that same
picture in the window we were once.
        I see us there behind the glass,
those fifteen years ago when we began.
        If I could snip their faces
out -- those candy-cane-smiled ones
        resembling friends on Christmas
cards we used to know. If I could paste
        our heads on their sure shoulders,
make our lives come true again.
        This once. Or, maybe
if I knew what she is saying sweetly
        to him, or perhaps her
recipe for burgundy beef stews, or
        even what detergent -- please --
what does she choose? How does
        she keep this picture moving,
with his arms around -- and snow
        outside?

YOU'RE GONE

Last year the moon rolled
    lightly over us,
and loving us,
    bounced roundly
up the dune. But this
    carved moon is
like a broken rocker rung,
    tossed out -- a slice
of smile that's tacked up,
    crooked, on the dark.

FROM A BIOLOGY TEXT

"Finning off, or slithering
through cool reeds,
these males left jelly
babies sloughed off --
just as all cold-blooded do."
Like skins of memory.

MADAME GAUGUIN -- LANDSCAPE

The house, he said,
    was drained of colors he had seen
there once. He left its dark
    for straw-bright summer seas.

The tenement behind her eyes
    locked memories of rooms inside --
once velvet with curved candlelight
    that marbled whispering on the walls.

Now her charades of them still ghost
    through upstairs halls, to listen
at the children's doors, their giggling
    and the little corks of apple munching.

Yet, the window-lights, knocked out,
    look blankly out
on yellow sky and fishbone
    trees, hooked into snow.

DISCIPLINES IN A WHITE BED

Love
was where the songs were written, where
she used to live, where after storms of lost
pink petals, trees burned red
with apples.

Night snow, and the world had gone to sleep,
except the cat and maybe God.
She stared through dark where love was once,
sat up in her white bed and turned her head
away, defended with her disciplines,
like beads to say, repeated recipes to:

> drift a salad wild with parsley,
> Poke a pitcher stiff with zinnias,
> Frost the sun with cotton curtains,
> Pulley picnics to the tree house.

She had said, aloud, that love was less
a place to live than any one of these.
She told herself each night --
although she always dreamed
the orchards
pink.

THE SWING

Somewhere I could almost hear my mother
    calling out across the years,
the backyard fence, to our rope swing, "Come in.
    It's time. You'll go outside
tomorrow. Hop out now and let
    the old cat die."

And like a hammock tilting
    in the wind, our cat tipped
sideways when I called her
    to come up the stairs.
She followed -- lightly touching fur
    against the velvet chair and moving
like a candle flame that gives
    its meaning to the dark,
belonging everywhere she walked
    this last, slow time.

Up in the rumple of my bed, I rounded
    her. I was her wicker basket
on this night. She was as slim as gothic
    saints, grown small on fasting --
yet, it was the cancer
    made her "pious," twisting her away
from cornflakes and sweet cream she used to
    lick so slyly from my bowl --
those foamy asterisks on her whiskers
    And her haunches stood out -- awkward
as a pair of earmuffs. Still, the web
    that wove her bones together
seemed too sprung to hold so round a purr.
    It scraped against an edge
somewhere; she coughed -- her breathing
    splintered with small whispers.

Now, although she seemed carved down
    to silent stone, a kitten sphinx, her airy
spirit floated -- light as ancient balsa wood
    that carried men across lost seas.
She put her paw across my wrist and let
    it rest there like dry snow upon
an oak leaf. She kept me and kept my hand
    from writing -- looking straight inside.
Her eyes were steady as blue stars
    that peer light-years deep into
telescopes to study old astronomers
    who watch. She knew.

THE PAINTING

April
bursts green
through the picture
growing in our
window.
Once,
we used to
watch at six
o'clock far down
the block
as fathers --
in Brooks Brothers'
suits with brief
cases -- walked
into spring
and into our
own leaf-
lace frame
of home --
coming,
the way we thought
it should be painted.

Stripes of sun
light shivering
across the grass
to children
playing catch
the father
of your choice
and bring him in
for tuna casserole
in candle light
in time for bed-
time stories we would
wind around and through
our arms and fingers,
thatching colors
in a basket, round
enough to hold us all
together
in that picture
no one dares
to look for now -- except
sometimes in April.

DOLPHIN

She leaves
      her shadow
swimming after her,
      fins free of time.
The water is her open
      window.

Jump! Then geysering
      tall, she quackly
laughs, a Disney voice,
      and takes the fish.

Wise speech professors
      puzzle-out her swerves
to translate into verbs.
      She grins. If that
amuses them, all right.
      They read the water
for her alphabet.
      She smiles, chin-up,
and travels in herself.
      She swims no fear
and has no tooth
      for hate.

She lets the trainer make
      believe she is his
faithful dog. He
      fetches for her --
making carnivals
      with balls and hoops.

She'll be his sea-lab
      Labrador to rescue men
or bombs, or pilot them through her
      moon-world of waterflowers --
all for fun of playing
      at the game of being man.

ROOKERY

The snow is blank white for a thousand
    miles. Don't ask me why our weather
copters landed on this arbitrary
    edge of ice. But penguins found
it first, aeons ago -- ancestral
    upstream mating rock
for tribes of trudging, shushing,
    mushing fishie-birds.

Our copters spotted them loop-sliding
    through the water in long chains.
They steadied on like pilgrims out across
    grim snow. Their nests were ritual
circles made of pebbles tottering from their beaks.
    Cartoons of us, they bartered for the rocks.

No one expected that our military base
    should move its garbage dump
because this bunch of balkie birds
    was targeted by genes,
predestined toward this
    hallowed, loving-ground of theirs.
They'd have to think new charts
    inside their heads if they
expected to have quiet snow
    and careful rims of rock to drop
their wobbly eggs in. But, not here --
    unless they wanted trouble.

What they wanted was their long
    Antarctic summer day --
on this plateau of snow and ceremony
    where they had belonged
since their first ancestor had tunneled
    from the egg and into sun here.

Sometimes penguins nearly froze,
    bent, lamed against
the winds, left standing --
    stonehenged in the storm.
But when snow stopped, their circle

eyes blinked open and they bobbled
off -- their tiny twig-wings stretching --
crippled crosses, skating ice.

We laughed at penguin babies, fat
balloons of slouchy pouch.
Their clicking tick-ticked, knocking
anxiously against their mothers'
beaks to beg for slippery swallowed
soups till they were gullet-full.

We watched each fuzzy head tilt back,
his beak a telescope that pointed up.
Or, like a finger drawing lines
across the sky -- connecting
all the stars with long cats-cradle-
strings that laced inside
his brain -- to tell him here was his
own space in time and place.

But men got tired of watching out
for clumsy birds. No signs to make way —
"Penguins Crossing." They were
trampled, stomped, and shoveled
into frozen heaps -- an Auschwitz,
bleeding bright cranberry ice.

Those that were left moved single file across
the snow, back into their long
night till next November -- never
doubting their ancestral-pull
that leads them over garbage to this valley
black, not knowing why
this grey snow makes them sick.
    They'll slowly hobble off, and yet
their eyes have no "Why's"
    in them -- only old, tried ways
to rock a nest, sit wisely on an egg.
    They are obedient to destiny, as sure
as their cats-cradle-stars. Men have divorced
    them from their place on this
white planet, but it still is theirs.
    This is the rookery.

LOCKED SHUTTERS

He
came calmly -- sunlight
through locked shutters --
factual, declarative,
a simple sentence. He
became cut-paper sun
striped down across
her shoulders making
ribbons wishes of her arms
and chalking long, bright
fingers like a staff that waits
for music.

She
will never open them or break
the lines of treble clef that tremble
down across her blouse. She'll
watch whole notes of elm
leaves fall against the shutters
shadowing music, playing
him.

CHURCH BENCHES

"I'll take you home," he said, just flat and twang,
a skillet brought down sharp against the stove.
His jaw clamped wire lips straight between and held
them tight as if he knew that it was less

a generation standing there between
them, more a state of understatement of
their eyes. They rode oak-stiff like church benches
and spoke in rote responsive readings, till

his hand touched her. "I'm awkward as a boot,"
he said, "and yet, I wanted you along."
Blue gingham bonnet, morning-glory sure,
she felt like Sunday School when church lets out --
kids laugh, and then God opens all the doors.

AN OLD LOVER DIES

The church is nearly empty. I'm alone
    far in the back -- like rain
blown in a window someone
    carelessly forgot.

His flowers turn to paper,
    music only water,
while the scripture webs above,
    pulls all of us together. His

girlfriend sits up in front -- proprietary
    prim -- and blinking. She does not know
she is just a cut-out playing me, while I
    am running through the rain, away.

WOULD HE STAND STILL FOR THIS

one
not so
soft kiss --
maybe violet-
size pressed slant-
wise
just for new
times's sake
this once
upon an afternoon
of dandelion sun
and sandwiches
that weren't as much
a picnic as that
apple-bite-together-
knowing-nothing
is
as real as
hidden life
lines rivering across
the pulse caught
at his neck?

He guessed
he might.

THE MAN WITH POET'S EYES

Where
is his old-dented-
hat smile -- painted
there as if some girl
had kissed him slant?
His twisted hold-
together belt grips
onto rumpled straw
legs in his knee-
thinned pants.

He is board-strong
and scarecrow-
tall, afraid
of nothing
more
than frightening
away the sparrows
or the crows.

They all come fluttering.
He waves
his long plaid
sleeve for them
to perch on,
each one chirping
to his blue glass
eyes the sky
sees through.

UNCOLLECTIBLE

From France he'd brought a magnum
    of champagne -- to watch it sparkling
through the stems of lovely girls, he said.
    Wine kindled far behind her eyes.

The railroad routes traced on his wall map
    showed where he had been, collecting.
Cities were dense vertices of wiggled
    lines -- like hair that marks erogenous
zones, those tiny lines converging, making
    x's, "showing subtly where the sex is."

Then he started with her shoulders, slowly
    coaxing her unfolding as if opening up
a map -- and geographically naive enough
    to think that all roads led to Rome.

ZOOLOGY PROFESSOR
Proof: "Ontology recapitulates philogeny."

He touched, asserted, opened her
    and read her all the way
back through her
    last divorce, regressing
her down to her dim beginnings —
    from her wound tight
babies borne, the bite-red
    burning hymen broken, past
her early longing, lily-deep,
    the hard bar-bruise
against her brother's bike
    when she was only ten --
back past her birth and amnions
    from there to aeons where
she gilled sweet guiles and flipped
    a flirting dorsal fin
through sperm and deep
    sea fern.

EXECUTIVE -- INTERNATIONAL

Business was his town; and it had moved with him
    from rural Sangamon on to Saigon.
Also the woman -- everywhere he knew her,
    dancing in the same black dress
cut low, her neck a slit of light,
    moon-cold, until he'd traced it,
opened up the dark. Then always,
    half-surprised, he found those moons --
as warm as barn-milk -- scooped
    from spilling buckets with his
hands, barns more than twenty
    years away from this Saigon.

At night he could discover
    her in any Hilton on the map --
until sleep slipped between
    them, shyly over them, and covered
them with modesty, returning
    him to his blonde wife --
left somewhere back
    in Wilmette, Illinois.

THE GIVER'S TALE

Once-upon-a-time her prince stole tarts
    their sugar grinning on his smile.
For him, she'd gathered sunshine
    on a string for curtains. Birthed
and jingled babies, rich as apples --
    learned to juggle budget-
algebra like oranges. Her hands
    worked mundane Tuesday miracles.

But he, and later, their grown children
    left. There weren't any presents
she could quite remember how to make.
    She bought a ticket on a train
and let it scream its rails inside her head
    and shudder through her
till a wealthy stock broker
    rode next to her. His stories
took her everywhere he'd been.
    She did not sit there knitting
socks for him -- not any gifts at all.
    Yet, when he looked at her their train flew
oceans -- laughing through quaint villages
    for ever after.

SUEDE

"I don't know how, quite, but
    I want you in my life,"
he said, and made her know
    the wine he poured
brimful was meant. She took
    his dare and slapped his
nametag on her pantyhose, high up,
    and rode in his convertible, top down,
through summer dark -- as if she'd waited
    all through college, through her
children's college, her divorce, to be
    eighteen again. Why wasn't
that enough? It was, except -- the suede
    way that his words moved round
and over her admitted
    it was not.

TWA FROM DENVER

He was seven miles higher than that
mile-high city. His highball was higher than that.
But he hadn't decided to see her again
till his jet scored the clouds almost down
to the rock where the mountains thrust young
as he'd felt when he held her.
And stones rode the river's wild water,
that burned and boiled white as love's anger
between them. Remembering how he had dared
through the gorge of the rock's jutted stride,
he was sure he would see her. And see her.

HALF FAIR

Nose up, the plane gripped
    speed, sucked air,
held on. For dear life,
    she had often
flown with him -- a cut-
    rate fare, just part
of his expense account,
    and written off.

With power buckled,
    tight inside
his safety belt, he skimmed
    his *National Observer.*

She gauged miles they
    hovered over life
and counted clouds
    that smouldered
over mountains
    as they jolted
through long shadows
    into Sunday.

She measured his hand --
    two news-print columns
wide, and one reach
    longer than her own.

A crinkle of grey curls
    crowded his collar.
Words chucked deep inside
    the husk of his moustache.
He squinted her inside his grin.
    All's fair in love.

Her blue silk nightgown had
    been stowed inside the cockpit,
sleeping in her suitcase as the plane
    notched down the sky.

UPON A WINTER TIME

Willows sprung,
    ribs belly-up against the amber
evening, and nothing moving
    but their car -- tick-tocking down
the exit ramp -- stretched like the second-
    hand around a clock.

He drove through snow, impatient
    plumes of speed burned through
the wind and smoldered into cold,
    no smiling in his eyes.

They stopped to see a Clock Museum --
    one great ark to house the archetypal
history of Time unwilling to get lost,
    tossed out with middens of the past.
Men had assigned these clocks
    to keep their time -- and send it
ticking, swinging, gonging out past
    death into a century without them.
Glass domed gears that cogged equations
    of sprung time. Minute
machines made pictures of the tinkering
    going on inside the heads of men.

He walked away, while she watched
    in a mirror, studying golden
hours etched on silver, helmeted with chimes.
    His boulder head could rock back
in a sudden laugh and set the whole
    museum donging, but it didn't.

Should she let him be time-keeper
    of her days -- collecting
secret seconds, weighing porcelain
    minutes, ringing castles of bright bells?
Not sure. She felt the brusque tweed
    of his jacket on her shoulders.

"Let me take you out of time, Love, light years
    far from calendars on stone," he laughed,
"and birds locked in their Swiss Chalets of music
    boxes." They moved toward the door
and into star time where the moon filled night
    and bedrooms with blue sleep.

FLIGHT

Then his suitcases carried him off --
    into sky, past the ports
of recalling the hushed touch
    of her whom he kept in his shadow —
away from his family-wife, left
    terrafirmly attached to her
Saturday calendar, forty-eighth parallel,
    speaking North platitudes.

Now he was free, gave himself
    to the sky. Was of air.
And the flying like dying -- without
    a decision to give
himself back, and not even
    to come down to either, or earth.

THE PRINCES

The slim-
lipped frogs jumped
quickly
slipping
into spring-
sprung knees.
They lost
themselves
inside a
circle sea
until the
shallow
ocean-suck
of sung-out
song re-
turned
them to the
frogs they
dreamed
they
weren't
on that
royal
night.

CALL NUMBERS 811.54

He phoned her from L.A.
"You are so understanding,
kind. You're right, I loved
my wife once too, the kids,
but, oh, the prison of those years
of working, chained to her,
that house. She never
valued me -- the way you do . . ."

Men often told her this,
their voices hovering.
She, smiling glassly,
listening to her own husband
somewhere, those same words
he'd whisper into younger ears.

And everyone became an echo. Sounds
anonymous, divorced from those
who shifted, nameless, under them --
world out of synchrony --
with no one owning homing
words that feathered close,
and no belonging to old promises,
or even to their old umbrellas --
and no linking who they were
on Tuesday with next Friday. Yet,
perhaps this grand mal was an earth-
fault some frail outer geo-
logic band had snapped and shifted,
misplaced people twenty-seven
counter-clock degrees
and wrenched them from their lives.

Then all the arms that reached to arms
let go at once, and all fell down,
each landing in another life,
two decibels beyond recall
of that old script -- the lies they used

to mean. And yet, they walked through new
routines, not noticing the change --
or if they almost did, relaxing on a fifty-
minute couch. Then mixing drinks and metaphors,
they ran zig-zag, coats open, shouting
songs but losing words and buttons
no one quite remembered why to sew on anymore.

"Remember last year when you phoned me
from L.A.?" she asked. "You didn't really hear my
voice. Though we could not admit it then.
The earth had shifted. Now all women have become
the same. We rotate past. Repeat.
I am the wife you left -- except this time
my eyes are brown."

Jaw clenched, he stared at her. "Don't
tell me that, Goddam! I'm free!
Don't haunt me with her voice. She never
understood, just used my life up.
Now her voice again inside my head.
She is becoming you! Shut up!"

He shoved his fist against her
mouth and rammed her words
like broken teeth into her throat.
He sent words screaming through
her, flying out her fingers,
getting lost in her old type-
writer, inside a book,
with call numbers that everyone
forgot. 811.54.

IN HIS DEN

She dusts his big brown desk
    that's sleeping like a bear
beneath a year's old papers,
    waiting to wake up, to sort
themselves, be stamped or filed
    or blown away.
Although he won't come home, she puts
    a clay pot ripe with crocuses, against
his stack of reference books -- no longer
    asked to refer anyone to anything.

She looks a word up in his leather dictionary,
    springs it free to fly out of the ark
of waiting-to-be-asked-for. Which dove?
    Which one? An "A" or "B" -- yes "Bear
Ursus Americanus, shaggy and omniverous —
    or man, especially burly, gruff . . . "

She almost sees him there, humped-curved
    inside his cave, and chuffled up in fur,
teeth gnawing off the sleeping edge
    of his old dreams to walk
upright, to be a man -- yet, be
    a brawly bear, take what he wants,
uncare. He scoops a fist of acorns
    then claw-combs a stream for fish,
and pads away -- a laugh chucked in
    his easy jaws. Sly tongue larps out
the side, a smile; a hard hug there for
    anyone inside his arms, with big bear
all around. Inside his supple bear
    suit, nonchalant, he hides
his running-speed should he decide
    to leave. Yet, if he left, he might
return, wake up in spring, stretch out
    his hulking arms, draw in his mate
and cubs, and yawn at day -- shake off
    the dusty paper leaves, begin again.

HER ULYSSES WISH

On a street of houses -- each a grave
    where someone lived,
she shuttered up her days
    remembering rambled years
of roses -- porcelain wth sun --
    elms sauntering shadows, sweet bees
smouldering through the blur of grass.
    Her yard was sagging under winters
of snow-faded leaves.
    One day she thought she heard him
swing the bent gate open, leave
    his leather briefcase in the hall.
Perhaps he'd brought her ginger cakes and crocuses,
    would talk till moonlight melted dark
and wrens were springing songs
    across the grey roof of the morning.

IF RAIN COULD STOP

The lake is sucking up the outboard motor sounds;
    the beer cans off the pier gulp sand.
You tell me I can wait down in the library --
    while birches outside swallow white
slim light that slips into the earth straws
    skimming sky down through their roots.
You bring some books I gave you years ago,
    dismiss me neatly as I walk into the rain.

Rain slopes along the brim of my old hat. It chases
    rivers down the road. "Wait up!" you call
and bring the bent umbrella from the hall. Then thunder;
    there's a scenery-shifting going on up in our sky.
"You might need this," you say, as if to pay up
    all your overdue library fines. I want to ask why
you don't have a handful of your sun-warmed-pebble
    words to skip across the lake. Why have you now

forgotten that we lived inside this waterfall, picked
    buckets of bright blueberries? Fresh sun inside
a Mason jar of purple jam, high on the shelf. And once
    upon our time, you used to come in like a spaniel
from the rain and shake your shaggy words across
    the room. Your puns ran halfway to the lake with us,
and chuckled circles underneath the sagging
    pier. We waded, swam, you palming

like white waves, up high around my legs --
    our knees came bobbling up against the shallow
water lid like four white lily pads. The reedy
    grass wrote thin green lines along our arms
as ducklings feathered by, gulped sweet
    mosquitoes. When we ran, trees twisting past,
cold streams of wind close-fitted
    up against our skins like wet T-shirts.

But I've grown old as lichen waiting on a tree.
    I want to say, "What can I do? I can't
be young. I can't be her -- although I'm still
    the tight-thighed daughter of myself." And yet,
no one can tell the time quite anymore. I can't move
    over in your cave, rump round against
your mossy night. Except, perhaps, if rain
    could stop, we'd swing out on a limber limb

across the summer, with the fireflies snapping
    on and off above our lake, and down
through shrill pine fronds — the ferns
    could fall asleep around our eyes.

THE TARNISHING

Before she moves with slow October
       hours, swinging in a silver
web where wild geese ebb far
       trails across South sky
like shadows through her head;
       before the bumble hums of dying
zinnias and creak of crickets
       in her walking through
tart apple afternoons
       turned gold and rolled
out lightly flowered
       and piqued with nutmeg
twists; she wonders if he might
       run home someday — too late.

BEGINNING ANOTHER TAIL?

Do you suppose, back in the nucleus
    of time, we got together lizardly
beneath a leaf? And did we lick our lidless
    eyes with our long windshield-wiper
viper tongues -- before deciding to be still
    as sticks, glued one to one, and wrapped
with vines beneath a savage orchestra
    of rain? And did the rocks burst,
loud with water, growing fangs of torrent
    over us and gnashing on our pond?

And when the scalding mists scaled up the morning
    to the mountain's top, did we ride wildly
on our green bicycle legs across the molten moat
    to hide our hybrid eggs just as a lightning
tree fell down and stepped hard on the tail
    of our own private evolution?

Then, could we begin another tail, as lizards do,
    a story of our race toward being
civilized beneath the net of trees
    that held the moon inside our jingling
jungle night? And could we see ourselves
    between the atoms of that lizard moon?

THE PAST VISITS

His jet ripped sky, split fog,
on-course — its homing instinct.
He'd lost his direction, skimming storms
to risk his past — ready
or not.

The plane arced high and stuttered
"in between earth and eternity," he mumbled.
Clouds gouged shadows on the mountains
as he travelled years back
into days with kids —
his own.

This was his week
to be the father of his
grown-up children,
walking them across
the red brick history
of Williamsburg — almost
like being father
of his country, too.

He reached an awkward
arm out toward his son,
and fumbled for his daughter's hand.
July heat sprang up
all around them —
tall as grass in this two-
century graveyard, markers
hidden, bumped against.

He seemed to lose his balance
some, was jostled, leaning on
the cement cemetery wall.

"I guess the wall's a little
wobbly," he laughed, "but notice
how it's rounded
on the top? Must be
to let the ghosts climb over;
it won't tear their robes."

At their Jamestown motel
he turned the pages of his
daughter's Memory Book, not seeing —
sinking deep inside them, falling
down — as in a dried-up well.

He sighed, said he'd check
out the photos later,
pushed the book quick-closed.
A pouch of air poofed out
a picture of their mother,
sent it scuttling across
the floor — just like a mouse
squeaked from a crypt.

Damn her! Determined to be
there, to share. She'd have
the last word yet.

The kids. Yes, they were like her words.
She'd said each one of them —
all her idea. He didn't have to listen.

Fog horns through the ghost-walked mist.
Grey harbor lights
dented the dark — but night
without its compass — had no
dream to ride back home
to sleep.

MARRIED BRIEFLY, ONCE AGAIN

They ushered her next to her former
    husband, neatly -- just another
friend belonging to the bride.
    The sanctuary shaped around
them like a cup, or nest. Their own
    had toppled from its branch.
The twittering organ raining
    from the roof,
licked down the railings,
    tongued her emptiness — until
he coughed, exhaled her, crossing properly
    his pin-striped knees.

TO SARA, LEAVING FOR COLLEGE
-- From Her Cave-Mother

Your jeans and books and easel packed,
    I think I have been saying
this goodbye too long to tell you now.
    I am remembering the spring when you
were born. I walked through wind,
    uphill -- your foetus fingers
smoothing patterns on the cave walls
    where you'd lived through winter
dark. You'd warmed me round with your
    own separate fire, till April.

All those months before, I'd felt your shadow
    move through me at night, tongued
cherry suck of asking all day
    long while you grew hungry
for new days. You seemed a fern
    unrolling -- sleeping seedly sweet --
then pointing smallest leaves
    for elbows, knees, and seeing.
Now the cave's left -- pictures finished,
    dim as dreaming painted on its walls.

MARSUPIAL MOTHER

Oak leaves munching sunlight
    and the shrill days, long
with children's arms that twisted like blue
    morning glories up around
her shoulders. Clover
    bubbling in the grass.

Their yellow afternoons stretched
    shivering into trees --
with autumn making brushfires
    of new colors -- near
the water, hammocking slow,
    back and forth in reeds.

Boats chafed against the shore
    and teased the children years away,
while maple leaves burned
    sugar smoke of childhood
they were sure they could row back
    to -- just two meadows on the left.

Time webbed the turn. Children forgot.
    Dark house. Her silver key snips
in the lock of her colonial box --
    each room upstairs a small museum
where the phones don't talk. She keeps
    three clovers in her pocket.

SIGNATURE

She seldom wore her glasses
      anymore, could hardly see the cat
up on "his" emptied desk across the room,
      and when she wrote her last name,
halos blotted all the e's
      and hammocks wrinkled underneath the W.

The watery hieroglyphs of that name
      he had left her with seemed quite unreal.
Then she got used to seeing letters
      half-osmosed into the paper,
only veins of ink-blue
      seafoam left.

She wondered if the cat
      had grown too old
to notice that her lap
      was tilting down;
small edges of her knees
      and ankles disappeared.

Her phone forgot to ring; she left
      her rolled up *Tribune* on the lawn.
Her mailbox had begun
      to call her "Occupant."

RIDING BACKWARD

Her bus rocked, sleepy as a waiting
    room on wheels. Her window flicked
fast movies passed, reversing
    days to summer years
and stopping them -- the slides
    of lives she'd lived.

The August trees held tight to wind
    and kept it tethered, then let go,
and left it wilting in the grass, just
    at the two-lane turnoff -- and
her house-that-used-to-be inside
    this rural see-through town
the highways all forgot --
    with sidewalks where nobody
walked -- where all the shades
    were pulled down on her childhood.

Yet, there, sandwiched somewhere in between
    McDonald's and the K-Mart -- home,
and she could almost hear the cattle moaning
    and the soybeans rattle.

DEEPER WATER

She'd driven hours home -- was lost
    inside the skull of time, looking for him.
The day did not move -- wedged
    there, held between
the crank-up beds, their tents of oxygen,
    the amber catheters in place.

That melting territory of her father's bones
    was huddled under fluttered
sheets. His sleeping mountain
    was arranged in pillows
of warm snow in range-grey blankets.
    He lay like the legendary Snowy Cross,
carved high in rock for tourists
    to remember Christ and pain. Too high
for him to breathe. He sucked thin air, let go.
    The crucifixion bird flew far away.

She reached out, touched his cold
    hard feet, uncovered them --
remembering when she was five, her yellow
    inner tube wound twice around.
She'd paddled after him, held tight with one
    hand to his toes. He'd floated out
to deeper water. She was scared. "Kick — kick,"
    he'd said, "I'm here. You'll be all right."

THE VISIT

Bound for winter, down the Illinois,
    moon-frozen backroads --
she drove through the pre-dawn dark,
    past flickering Bethlehems
toward Christmas-card-blue sky
    and her once holly-eyed young mother.

Though no holidays were left
    downstate or anywhere, she drove
toward day, the color of cool dust,
    through sleeting rain, slant grey
as wood-grained barns, to visit
    in the cemetery of her childhood.

Stretched miles ached across the prairie loam,
    no longer briared with blackberries.
Big agribusiness had smalled down
    the hills and shallowed over valleys,
broken fences, flattened dirt, tamped
    down the farms with pickup trucks.

Why was she always stuck behind a truck?
    Someone inside -- inside a cowboy hat.
The houses huddled under prairie storm
    like white-faced heifers. Once,
strong corn and wheat and kids were raised
    on farms, but no one's left there now.
The farmers sold their land as easily as
    they stomped the thick mud off their boots.

She watched birds settle in the rasping
    husk of paper fields to wait
for sky break and slow amber morning --
    then to fly away like words.

The edge of town, the quiet place,
     she stopped -- her fingers prying at
the stiffened snow to find the marker
     where her father slept
with stories locked inside, and next
     to him her little sister.

When she jabbed a pencil through the ice
     to anchor in a wreath of cranberries
and pine, she smoothed the snow —
     like scribbling words across their pillow.

FLOWERED APRON

Although radishes were always much
    too strong, I grabbed
a bunch to take along and tossed my suitcase
    in the car. My father used to kid
that radishes were Mother's "favorite fruit."
    When he'd been there the two of us
teamed up, teased her.
    I gnawed a radish, let it crisp my teeth
and numb my tongue -- as if it made me know
    her better -- now that she was needing
me. From my fern porch, the road would lead two hundred
    miles to her slim bed -- now solemn with "the tied-down
sheets," a nurse said on the phone. I drove too fast
    inside the gap of wind and raced against the furrow
of a storm, where rain turned grass to gullies,
    swallowed into rivers. Clouds stampeded
hard across the fields of Illinois where half
    the world's corn bread was growing.
Wide wind pushed my car, bent back a small bird's wings
    and caught it struggling like a stroke inside the sky.

Then sun -- and calm soup-kettle ponds, vanilla
    smell of fields, and locusts humming like machines
that milled the wheat till night turned silk with city
    lights, and I was there. Yet not.

She mumbled, "No, that's not my girl,"
    and turned away. Like summer wind, her hair
frayed out across her pillow. Words rolled round
    inside her head, her eyes were skating circles
as she mined her head for words to tell herself
    that she was still alive. She spoke
as if a priest had pressed a wafer
    to her tongue. "Dearie, you came!" she said.

"She's always cresting on a flood of facts,"
  my father often told me, frowning some,
"and yet that bright head never drowns in them."
  Now all she needed was a seldom word
bobbed up and watery as communion wine, the splash
  of each one new upon her lips, sweet lick to taste.

At her apartment I tried on her flowered apron, crisp
  as ruffled curtains. When I phoned long-distance-
cousins, I could hear her voice echo
  my own -- my mother stuck inside my head,
glued tight. Then later, as the crickets rocked the night
  to sleep on rusty springs, I thought
how long she'd waited for her turn --
  her being first and most important, calling
all the apples on our family tree to come, those apples
  rolling down into her flowered apron, home.

DIRECTIONS FOR ENJOYING RAISIN BREAD

When the clouds are cherry
    trees in blossom
and the wind is April rivering
    through your blouse,
walk down a winding road where grass
    is tame and furred up close.

Be sure to take a soft-baked
    loaf along to Dreamland
Pond for calling ducks.
    They'll vee across to you
where grackles glisten on the rocks
    and flutter over crumbs.

Now, gnaw a yeasty bite yourself, then
    throw the bread upon the water.
Even catfish, sprouling their curled
    whiskers, will gulp slices of this
sweet life raft and kiss the raisins
    speckling on their water lid.

THE SUN-WORSHIPPER AND THE CAT

Through sunlight years the mop and scouring
    sponge have curled my fingers.
Tools have glued their work and purpose
    to my hands. I'm one of them.
I worship highlights shining in the pewter teapot,
    subtle golds released from polished wood.

Today my knees dent into floor
    tiles, pray them sudsy clean.
I lean back, sitting stiffly while
    the cat climbs up, claims I
have made a lap for him. He gently
    staples me in this madonna-like
cat-cradling pose. Or, he will be my zither,
    humming as he humors me and lets
me strum his ribs and smooth his
    frets. He squints a smile at me,
then to the sun that slides out of the clouds
    and slips down through the window
in a shimmer -- as if kneeling at his
    feet -- on my bright kitchen floor.

GIRL PAINTED INTO A WHEATFIELD 1547 A.D.

Today is mine and sun in me
while I lie down inside
this honey lake of grass.
It whispers all around me, leaning in --
as if I were just born and lying in a crib.
Warm cider bubbles in my head,
my hair is hazy in the wind.

I stretch out on this last loaf
of the sun-filled field to touch
the twisting end of summer.
Sun is buttering me all yellow --
melting, tickling slowly down
into my ears. Wind shivers up
my knees and underneath my apron skirt.

The sun is drizzling bees around my grape-
bunched toes, while pigeons shuffle squeaking
wings above my head. The sheep munch close
where crickets prickle quiet. I am caught
by sleep — as stiff as any toad found
in December. Then wind Breughels over me, unlaces
ribbons on my bodice, paints me pink and gold.

The sun is reaching back, reciting
history to me of all my many
mother-selves-ago. Then wind clouds
shallow sky, shake apples, bumping
to the grass -- while I jump up to step
across the gilt-edged frame to join
the gallery tour, my life.

PRAIRIE CHICKEN

Husband, children flown, she sat there
    on the land her father left her
like a nutmeg, custard-colored hen
    all ruffled out and feathering in
around the slightest pretext of a baby
    chick, or piping duckling, or
a china "doorknob" knocked out
    of the turkey trough.

Broods hatched, she fluttered up
    to perch, thonged into that old
sticker-juniper out by the porch --
    its branches threshing wind.

She looked out past the string
    of sparrows ravelling down
the sky and knew that this
    whole prairie was her nest —
sat there blink-eyed through rain, soft-
    clucking to the feathery snow.

WRITING BY ROTE

The miles had rumbled storms
    around my tires,
wound into me and circled
    through my arms.
I held the steering wheel
    with my left hand
and "drove" the Magic Marker
    with my right -- across
the notebook next to me, while I watched
    traffic. Words came quivering
through my fingers, speeding blind —
    all by themselves.

What gradeschool teacher printed
    those deep circuitries inside my Palmer
Method scrawl? Miss Emerson --
    the one who stood before us
like a pair of scissors pasted shut.
    Her hair was waved in light
blue ink-script "m's," and braided
    into "x's" in the back.

Her pointing stick snapped smartly
    on the flesh-pink wall map
named Brazil -- a big palm print,
    its heart-line running
riverly across and called
    the Amazon, where women
wore their hair in rivers, down
    across their sun-warm breasts.

Miss Emerson had pointed to the bump
    on my third finger, smiled,
"You know," she said, "you're just
    like me; we hold the pen
too tightly. See?" She moved
    my arm. "You must relax --
push-pull, push-pull. You'll make that w —

a squirrel that hops, falls down,
     hops up again across the fence.
          You see?"

And even now, sometimes, while writing "w,"
     I chant, "falls down, hops up."
Miss Emerson had let me sponge the blackboards
     that day — long, grey push-pull strokes.

My car slowed down, the slate sky
     cracked; rain blurred blank white,
then streaked in chalk lines. Wind
     pulled hard against my toy-sized
car. I drove the wobbled storm rim,
     both hands gritted-tight around
the wheel. My car smacked flat
     against the concrete median, let go,
went sliding through a sky as green
     as hills of Oz -- "Oh, Auntie Em,
Where are you now?
     And Kansas?
And Miss Emerson?" Trees twisted
     into "l's." My car was push-
pulled, set down neatly in between
     the yellow lanes lines.

Rain had stopped, trees lifting
     sky up. Sun was scraped
against the storm. The wind
     slapped light like yellow
tempera paint across my car,
     spilled dandelions in the grass.

"Miss Emerson, where have you
     gone? Have you been
buried under forty years
     of chalk dust? Or, are
you rolled up inside Brazil's
     pink river heart-line --
tightly saved inside the second
     grade's scroll map?"

COLOR OF HOME

When I was eight, Chicago was the world
    the newspapers made real
as movies; and we'd pay to go
    to see it on the train
from downstate Illinois, where nothing
    happened much -- except
when we, like frozen mittens,
    tumbled in the snow down Lincoln's
courthouse hill. Or, in the spring,
    we looked for May apples
and waded streams that jingled
    blue inside our bones.

On any day, I would have traded
    my town's maple streets
for rainbow windows framing
    Michigan Avenue -- and people walking
brisk as nine o'clock -- the "L," electric
    in their steps. When deep Chicago cold
creased in around my handknit scarf,
    my parents bought us cherry sweetrolls,
hot. We munched and walked twelve blocks
    to feast on summer color at the art museum.

Later, bride-young, lavender in love
    in my Chicago, galleries served up
art -- caught melon-ripe and sliced, a glint
    of juice dripped down the rind.
Few artists painted with blue cobwebs.
    Rather, blades of color -- wild
as windmills. But one canvas trembled
    like a tulip, fragile clams of petal
pink that wanted to be opened up.
    "Too soon," my lover said.
And yet, I asked him to shift sunlight --
    be the cubist, cut small wedges
from my eyes and glue them back
    a different way to see.